AMERICA TRIUMPHS

THE STORY OF OUR HEROES

FROM 9/11 TO THE DEMISE OF BIN LADEN

MARY BOONE

TRIUMPH®
BOOKS

This book is available in quantity at special discounts for your group or organization. For further information, contact:

Triumph Books
542 South Dearborn Street
Suite 750
Chicago, Illinois 60605
(312) 939-3330
Fax (312) 663-3557
www.triumphbooks.com

Printed in U.S.A.

ISBN: 978-1-60078-673-0
Content developed and packaged by Rockett Media, Inc.
Writer: Mary Boone
Editor: Bob Baker
Design and page production: Andrew Burwell

Photographs courtesy of Getty Images unless otherwise noted

AMERICA TRIUMPHS

04 INTRODUCTION

06 CHAPTER 1:
THE DAY

38 CHAPTER 2:
OSAMA BIN LADEN AND AL-QAEDA

74 CHAPTER 3:
HUNTING A TERRORIST

96 CHAPTER 4:
THE NATION, WORLD REACT

112 EPILOGUE

AMERICA TRIUMPHS

Osama bin Laden, long hunted as the mastermind behind the worst terrorist attack ever to occur on U.S. soil, was killed May 1, 2011, by U.S. forces.

President Barack Obama announced the news in a rare late-night press conference, calling the killing the "most significant achievement to date" in the effort to defeat al-Qaeda.

"Justice has been done," a somber President Obama told the American people.

The battle had been grueling, but this was an undeniable triumph over evil.

Bin Laden's greatest triumph was one of America's darkest days: Sept. 11, 2001.

On that morning, al-Qaeda terrorists hijacked four commercial jets. The hijackers crashed two of the airliners into the Twin Towers of the World Trade Center in New York City, killing everyone on board and many others working in the buildings. The hijackers crashed a third airliner into the Pentagon. The fourth plane crashed into a field near Shanksville, Pennsylvania, after some of its passengers and crew attempted to regain control of the plane, which the hijackers had redirected toward Washington, D.C.

There were no survivors from any of the flights. Nearly 3,000 victims died in the attacks.

There had been terrorist attacks before. But this one – this one was bigger and more personal than any before it. If bin Laden thought 9/11 would cripple America, he was sorely mistaken. Instead, the attacks galvanized this country's citizens. It didn't matter their age, the color of their skin, their political affiliation, or how much money they earned. Americans wanted Osama bin Laden to pay for his crimes against their nation.

An evil genius, bin Laden eluded capture for nearly a decade. When U.S. Navy SEALs finally found and executed the terrorist, Americans responded with emotions that ran the gamut from pure elation to national pride to fear of retaliation.

Peace had triumphed over terror. Justice had triumphed over injustice. And good had triumphed over evil.

'JUSTICE HAS BEEN DONE'

U.S. forces kill Osama bin Laden

PRIVILEGED SON BECAME THE GLOBAL FACE OF TERRORISM

BY BRADLEY GRAHAM

Osama bin Laden, 54, who was born into Saudi riches, only to end up leading a self-declared holy war against the United States as head of one of the most ruthless, far-flung terrorist networks in history, died Sunday in the manner he had often predicted: in a strike by U.S. forces.

As the founder of al-Qaeda, bin Laden demonstrated the power and global reach of a terrorism campaign rooted in centuries-old Islamic beliefs and skilled in modern-day technologies. The militants he inspired have proved surprisingly resilient, and the organization he established continues to pose a substantial threat to U.S. interests overseas and at home.

Although bin Laden was able to elude an intense U.S. manhunt for years, al-Qaida's ranks were increasingly weakened by the capture or killing of senior operatives.

Further, his violent mission never came close to achieving its central aims of pushing U.S. forces out of the Middle East and toppling U.S.-backed Arab gov-

GETTY IMAGES

PUBLIC ENEMY: Bin Laden was also wanted in al-Qaeda's bombings of U.S. embassies in Tanzania and Kenya in 1998.

REUTERS

HISTORIC: Bin Laden's death will provide a clear moment of victory for Obama at a time of deep political turmoil overseas.

TEAM ATTACKE COMPOUND IN PAKISTAN WHER HE WAS HIDING

BY SCOTT WILSON AND CRAIG WHITLOCK

Osama bin Laden has been killed in a U.S. operation in Pakistan, President Obama announced from the White House on Sunday, calling his death "the most significant achievement to date in our nation's effort to defeat al-Qaeda."

Speaking from the East Room, Obama said a small team of U.S. personnel attacked a compound Sunday in the city of Abbottabad, where bin Laden had been hiding since late last summer. After a firefight, the president said, the U.S. team killed bin Laden and "took custody of his body."

"We will be relentless in defense of our citizens and our friends and allies," a somber Obama said in his nine-minute statement. "We will be true to the values that make us who we are. And on nights like this one, we can say to families who have lost loved ones to al-Qaeda's terror: Justice has been done."

The killing of bin Laden — which drew a spontaneous, cheering crowd outside the White House

CHAPTER 1
THE DAY

CHAPTER 1: **THE DAY**

John Patrick O'Neill retired as the FBI's top terrorist expert in 2001. During his 31 years time with the FBI, O'Neill had worked on many of the world's deadliest terrorist attacks including the 2000 bombing of the USS Cole, the 1998 attacks on the U.S. embassies in Africa, and the

building.

"Val, it's horrible," he said. "There are body parts everywhere."

O'Neill also called his son and FBI headquarters before re-entering one of the World Trade Center towers to assist in the evacuation. He was inside the building

1993 truck bombing of the World Trade Center.

On August 23, 2001, O'Neill started a new job, as security director for the World Trade Center.

On September 11, 2001, O'Neill was in his 34th floor office in the World Trade Center's North Tower at 8:46 a.m., when American Flight 11 crashed into it. Once outside the building, he called a friend, Valerie James, to ask her what hit the

when it collapsed.

Within hours, it became clear that John O'Neill's death on September 11, 2001, came at the hands of terrorists. The 9/11 attacks, now known as the deadliest terrorist attack ever to take place on American soil, resulted in 2,996 deaths, including 2,977 victims and 19 hijackers. The dead included business people, members of the military, mothers, fathers and children from 90 different countries.

America Triumphs 9

911 Calls

Compassion and comfort was pretty much all New York City 911 operators could offer in the chaos that ensued on September 11, 2001.

Partial transcripts of that day's 911 calls were released in 2006, after media outlets and family members sued to have the information made public. The transcripts include only the voices of emergency operators —not civilian callers. These excerpts provide a glimpse into the horror of the day:

"I want you to go on the floor. Kneel on the floor. On the floor," said an operator.

"Listen to me, ma'am," an operator told a woman trapped on the 83rd floor of the World Trade Center. "You're not dying. You're in a bad situation, ma'am."

"Just sit tight. Just sit tight. We're on the way," a dispatcher says at 8:50 a.m.

"You saw an explosion at the twin towers?"

"He jumped out which window, which floor? Do you know?"

"OK, if you feel your life is in danger, do what you must do. I can't give you any more advice than that."

"They're saying it might be a terrorist attack. It would have to be, because what are the odds of two planes crashing into the same building, OK? ... OK. I can't believe this. It's got to be ... it's got to be hell."

"All I can tell you is to sit tight, because I have almost every fireman in the city coming out."

"I'm still here. The fire department is trying to get to you. OK, try to calm down."

"I understand your concern, sir, and I understand your panic, but we are there in the building. We're getting there as soon as we can."

The 8:46 a.m. attack that stirred O'Neill from his office was the first of four airline hijackings and suicide attacks committed against the United States that fateful day.

Nineteen militants associated with the Islamic extremist group al-Qaeda carried out the acts of terrorism. The hijackers, most of whom were from Saudi Arabia, had established themselves in the United States, many well in advance of the attacks. They traveled in small groups, and some of them received commercial flight training. On September 11, 2001, groups of attackers boarded four domestic aircraft at three East Coast airports. Soon after takeoff, they disabled the crews and took control of the planes. The aircraft, all large and bound for the West Coast, had full loads of fuel.

The first flight to crash originated from Boston. Roughly 15 minutes later, a second plane, United Airlines Flight 175, also from Boston, struck the World Trade Center's South Tower. Both structures were horribly damaged by the impact and erupted into flames.

A third plane, from the Washington, D.C., area, struck the southwest side of the Pentagon just outside the city at 9:40, touching off a fire in that section of the structure.

Within the next hour, a fourth plane, this one from Newark, New Jersey, plummeted into the Pennsylvania countryside after its passengers and crew tried to overpower their assailants.

At 9:59, the World Trade Center's heavily damaged south tower collapsed; the north tower fell about a half hour later. A number of other buildings adjacent to the twin towers suffered serious damage, and several subsequently fell. Fires at the World Trade Center site smoldered for more than three months.

The World Trade Center's towers—

known as the Twin Towers—had been one of New York City's most recognizable landmarks. Because of the towers' location within the largest city in the country, hundreds of thousands of people

THIS MEMORIAL IS IN MEMORY
OF THE BRAVE MEN AND WOMEN
WHO GAVE THEIR LIVES
TO SAVE SO MANY OTHERS.
THEIR COURAGE AND LOVE
OF OUR COUNTRY WILL BE
A SOURCE OF STRENGTH AND COMFORT
TO OUR GREAT NATION.
GOD BLESS AMERICA.

CHRISTIAN ADAMS
FLIGHT ATTENDANT LORRAINE G. BAY
TODD BEAMER
ALAN BEAVEN
MARK BINGHAM
DEORA BODLEY
FLIGHT ATTENDANT SANDRA W. BRADSHAW
MARION BRITTON
THOMAS BURNETT
WILLIAM CASHMAN
GEORGINE CORRIGAN
PATRICIA CUSHING
CAPTAIN JASON DAHL
JOSEPH DELUCA
PATRICK DRISCOLL
EDWARD FELT
JANE C. FOLGER
COLLEEN FRASER
ANDREW GARCIA
JEREMY GLICK
KRISTIN GOULD
LAUREN GRANDCOLAS
FLIGHT ATTENDANT WANDA A. GREEN
DONALD GREENE
LINDA GRONLUND
RICHARD GUADAGNO
FIRST OFFICER LEROY HOMER
TOSHIYA KUGE
FLIGHT ATTENDANT CEECEE LYLES
HILDA MARCIN
WALESKA MARTINEZ
NICOLE MILLER
LOUIS J. NACKE
DONALD PETERSON
JEAN PETERSON
MARK ROTHENBERG
CHRISTINE SNYDER
JOHN TALIGNANI
HONOR ELIZABETH WAINIO
FLIGHT ATTENDANT DEBORAH A. WELSH

UNITED FLIGHT 93
SEPTEMBER 11, 2001

Memorials

Ten years after the United States' worst terrorist attack, a memorial to its victims will be dedicated in New York City on September 11, 2011.

The 9/11 Memorial is located at the site of the former World Trade Center complex, and occupies approximately half of the 16-acre site. The 9/11 Memorial features two enormous waterfalls and reflecting pools, each about an acre in size, set within the footprints of the twin towers. Listed on the memorial will be the names of the 2,977 people killed in the Sept. 11, 2001, attacks in New York, Washington, D.C., and Pennsylvania; and the six people who died in the Feb. 26, 1993, bombing of the World Trade Center. The 9/11 victims are grouped on the memorial according to which flight they were on, whether they were first responders, worked at the Pentagon or were in one of the trade center towers.

Family, co-workers at companies located inside the trade center and first responders asked that certain victims' names be placed together, and the memorial's designers worked to accommodate them.

Meanwhile, Flight 93 National Memorial is transitioning from a temporary memorial into a permanent memorial. Phase 1 of the park-like memorial, located in rural Pennsylvania at the site of the crash, will be unveiled on the 10th anniversary of 9/11.

Known as the Field of Honor, visitors will enter the memorial through a clearing of trees on a black slate plaza marking Flight 93's path. The memorial design commemorates the collective act of courage by the 40 passengers and crew of Flight 93 through 40 Memorial Groves of Red and Sugar Maple trees in a shared, curving embrace of the Field of Honor's open space. The national memorial also includes a Tower of Voices containing 40 large wind chimes, evocative of, and a tribute to, the sound of the wind and voices aboard the plane during its final moments.

Pentagon Memorial was dedicated in September 2008; it was the first of the national 9/11 memorials to reach completion. A grooved, gray concrete wall rises from a few inches to a few feet. The wall is designed to remind visitors of the youngest and oldest victims, wrapping the memorial in symbolic imagery.

It stands 3 inches tall at its beginning, representing the youngest person killed there —3-year-old Dana Falkenberg—and continues to a height of 71 inches, corresponding to the oldest victim, retired U.S. Navy Capt. John D. Yamnicky Sr.

Many states and regions have constructed their own memorials to the victims of the 9/11 attacks. Additionally, permanent websites pay tribute to the victims so that America and Americans might never forget.

The Pentagon 9/11 Memorial.

witnessed the attacks. Millions of others watched the tragic event unfold on television.

Of the day's many horrific images, none was so haunting as the sight of those trapped in the upper levels of the tower who chose to jump to their deaths that morning. It's thought that at least 200 people jumped to their deaths, alone, in pairs, or in groups. Most jumped from the north tower's 101st to 105th floors, where the Cantor Fitzgerald bond firm had its offices, and the 106th and 107th floors, where a conference was being held. Others leaped from the 93rd through 100th floor offices of the Marsh & McLennan insurance company. Only a handful leapt from the south tower.

For those who jumped, the fall lasted less than 10 seconds. Traveling at around 150 miles per hour, the impact was enough to ensure death.

Rescue operations began almost immediately as the country and the world sought to come to grips with the enormity of the losses. Those losses were amplified as some of the very same workers who came to rescue victims became victims. The New York City Fire Department lost 341 firefighters and 2 paramedics. The New York City Police Department lost 23 officers. The Port Authority Police Department lost 37 officers, and 8 additional EMTs and paramedics from private Emergency Medical Service units were killed. In all, some 2,750 people were killed in New York, 184 at the Pentagon, and 40 in Pennsylvania.

The collective emotional distress of the four attacks was overwhelming. Throngs of people stricken with grief gathered at "ground zero"—as the site where the

Living in a Post-9/11 World

September 11, 2001, marked a turning point in American foreign and domestic policy.

On October 26, 2001, Congress passed the USA Patriot Act. The legislation dramatically reduced restrictions on law enforcement agencies' ability to search telephone, email communications, medical and financial records. It also eased restrictions on foreign intelligence gathering within the United States; expanded the Secretary of the Treasury's authority to regulate financial transactions, particularly those involving foreign individuals and entities; and broadened the discretion of law enforcement and immigration authorities in detaining and deporting immigrants suspected of terrorism-related acts. The act also expanded the definition of terrorism to include domestic terrorism.

New policies including the nation's "No-Fly List," crackdowns at borders, and surveillance of mosques and homes were just a few of the ways in which the nation's citizens saw government surveillance increase.

The United States Department of Homeland Security (DHS) is a cabinet-level department of the U.S. federal government, created in response to the September 11 attacks. With more than 200,000 employees, DHS is now the third largest Cabinet department.

Within two months of the September 11 attack, the Transportation Security Administration (TSA) was created as part of the Aviation and Transportation Security Act. The organization was charged with developing policies to protect U.S. transportation, especially in airport security. Security screening at American airports immediately became tougher. No more wearing your jacket and shoes through screening. No more liquids in your carry-on bag. Backscatter X-rays and sliding pat-downs became part of the pre-boarding drill in 2010.

While all these new policies and regulations were designed to make America a safer place, some of them also made the country a more divided and suspicious country. Arab, Muslim, Sikh, and South-Asian Americans—as well as those perceived to be members of these groups—have been the victims of bias-related assaults, threats, vandalism and arson. Air travelers have cried foul when pat-downs became too personal. Racial profiling has been labeled a discriminatory and ineffective law enforcement tool.

"September 11 was when we lost something. Not innocence, exactly. It wasn't simply the first dawning of tragedy in our lives. It was ... the one salient incident that indelibly altered the way we saw safety, privacy, probability," wrote *The Washington Post*'s Alexandra Petri. "It crystallized our characteristic, semi-contradictory generational attitude: optimistic fatalism."

towers once stood came to be known—some with photos of missing loved ones, seeking some hint of their fate. Others, some injured, others in shock, wandered the streets of the city, unsure how they

near the crash site, others working inside the Pentagon that morning did not know that a plane had hit their building. Military and civilian personnel ran up and down the corridors yelling for people to get out; their actions were credited with saving a lot of lives.

Mounted police make their way along an access road leading to the crash site of United Airlines Flight 93 through the early morning fog on September 12, 2001, in Shanksville, Pennsylvania.

Flight 93 was United Airlines' daily scheduled transcontinental flight, from Newark International Airport to San Francisco International Airport. On Tuesday, September 11, 2001, the Boeing 757-222 aircraft flying that route

would get home. Dust and smoke filled the air. Traffic wasn't moving. Subway lines were closed. Phone lines were jammed.

Just a few hours away, in Washington, D.C., American Airlines Flight 77 bound for Los Angeles was hijacked and crashed at 345 miles per hour into the west side of the Pentagon. All 58 passengers, four flight attendants, and both pilots on board, as well as 125 occupants of the Pentagon, died.

Although the blast from the plane and the toxic gas and heat from the resulting fire killed some people in their offices

was hijacked by four al-Qaeda terrorists, and subsequently crashed into a field.

Approximately 46 minutes into the flight, the hijackers breached the cockpit and overpowered the flight crew; Ziad Jarrah, a trained pilot, took control of the aircraft and diverted it toward Washington, D.C. It is thought the intended target was the U.S. Capitol or the White House. Several passengers and crew members made telephone calls aboard the flight and learned about the attacks on the World Trade Center and the Pentagon. As a result of this knowledge, the passengers

Emergency workers search the crash site of United
Airlines Flight 93 in Shanksville, Pennsylvania.

U.S. President George W. Bush (L) unveils the new postage stamp which uses the famous photo by Thomas E. Franklin of *The Bergen Record* of New York firefighters raising a flag at ground zero.

Indelible Image

When an editor at *The Bergen Record* (Passaic, New Jersey) told photographer Thomas E. Franklin a plane had hit the World Trade Center, Franklin jumped in his car and headed down the New Jersey Turnpike to Jersey City.

Franklin stopped at Exchange Place in Jersey City and went to the riverfront. He was a pro and he knew where the best views of the WTC would be.

Franklin put a memory card into his camera and started shooting: ferries carrying wounded persons, the establishment of a triage area, faces of area residents thankful to be away from the danger and death.

Around noon, another photographer convinced the police to let himself and Franklin take a tugboat to New York. As Franklin further penetrated Ground Zero, police threatened to arrest him about a half dozen times.

Franklin was traveling with James Nachtwey, a Pulitzer-Prize winning photojournalist who told him he had just narrowly escaped death at Ground Zero. A couple hours later, Franklin and Nachtwey were taking a break when a trio of firefighters caught Franklin's eye.

"I would I say was 150 yards away when I saw the firefighters raising the flag. They were standing on a structure about 20 feet above the ground. This was a long lens picture: there was about 100 yards between the foreground and background, and the long lens would capture the enormity of the rubble behind them," Franklin said.

The three firefighters, William Eisengrein, George Johnson and Daniel McWilliams, had discovered a U.S. flag on the back of a yacht near the World Financial Center. They decided to raise it as a statement of loyalty and resilience.

Franklin recalled, "I made the picture standing underneath what may have been one of the elevated walkways, possibly the one that had connected the World Trade plaza and the World Financial Center. As soon as I shot it, I realized the similarity to the famous image of the Marines raising the flag at Iwo Jima.

"This was an important shot. It told more than just death and destruction. It said something to me about the strength of the American people and of these firemen having to battle the unimaginable."

Franklin's photograph appeared in the September 12, 2001, *Record*. Reaction was swift and intense. *The Record* received 30,000 requests to reprint the photograph, which the paper initially granted if they were not for profit.

Later, the newspaper allowed reprint rights in return for donations to its disaster fund, which eventually swelled to $400,000. The money was distributed to charities selected by the firefighters in the photo. The photo eventually was made into an authorized poster sold through the paper's Web site and private companies.

At the end of 2001, the Associated Press Managing Editors Association and Editor & Publisher magazine named it the best picture of the year. The photo was on the short list of photographs considered for the Pulitzer Prize. A "Heroes 2001" stamp issued by the US Postal Service with the Franklin image was unveiled in the Oval Office in March 2002.

Franklin remains modest about the picture, saying that it was only by chance that he witnessed the firefighters.

"There were times during the day that I cried. Nothing had ever touched me as emotionally as this," Franklin said. "But I had a job to do ... Once I made deadline, all I wanted to do was see my wife and my son."

Military vehicles travel along the road leading to the crash site of United Airlines Flight 93.

united to mount an assault against the hijackers in an attempt to regain control of the aircraft.

The plane crashed in a field in near Shanksville, Pennsylvania, about 80 miles southeast of Pittsburgh and 150 miles northwest of Washington, D.C. Everyone on board was killed. The plane fragmented upon impact, leaving a crater, and some debris was blown miles from the crash site. Of the four aircraft hijacked that day, United Airlines Flight 93 was the only one that failed to reach its intended target.

Flights across the country were grounded for fear of another attack. World markets were shaken and damage to Lower Manhattan's infrastructure, combined with fears of stock market panic, kept New York markets closed for four trading days. When they reopened, markets suffered record losses.

Other countries and their leaders rallied in support of the United States. Evidence soon convinced most governments that the Islamic militant group al-Qaeda was responsible for the attacks. The group had been implicated in previous terrorist strikes against Americans, and its leader, Osama bin Laden, had made numerous anti-American statements. Al-Qaeda was headquartered in Afghanistan and had forged a close relationship with that country's Taliban militia, which subsequently refused U.S. demands to extradite bin Laden and to terminate al-Qaeda activity there. In October 2001, U.S. and allied military forces launched an attack that, within months, killed or captured thousands of militants and drove Taliban and al-Qaeda leaders into hiding.

Following the September 11 attacks, the U.S. government exerted great effort to track down other al-Qaeda agents and sympathizers throughout the world, and it made combating terrorism the focus of U.S. foreign policy. Meanwhile, security measures within the country were tightened considerably at such places as airports, government buildings, and sports venues.

The United States was badly bruised by the very event that galvanized it. Strangers united behind the red, white and blue. Prayers were said for strangers who lost loved ones. And Americans vowed not to rest until the man responsible for these atrocities was forced to pay for his actions.

U.S. Air Force Reservist Staff Sgt. Brian of the 93rd Bomber Squadron applys a decal with the phrase 'Lets Roll' to the side of a B-52 bomber February 20, 2002 at Barksdale Air Force Base in Louisiana.

Let's Roll

Todd Beamer, a 32-year-old account manager for the Oracle Corporation, was one of 40 individuals who died on United Airlines Flight 93 on September 11, 2001,

Beamer is survived by his wife, Lisa Beamer, two sons, David and Drew, and a daughter, Morgan Kay, who was born nearly four months after her father's death.

Beamer was one of many of the Quiet Heroes of 9/11.

He and other passengers had been in communication with people via in-plane and cell phones and learned that the World Trade Center had been attacked using hijacked airplanes. Beamer tried to place a credit card call through a phone located on the back of a plane seat but was routed to a customer-service representative instead, who passed him on to supervisor Lisa Jefferson.

Beamer was able to report that one passenger was killed and, later, that a flight attendant had told him the pilot and co-pilot had been forced from the cockpit and may have been wounded.

He was also on the phone when the plane made its turn in a southeasterly direction, a move that had him briefly panicking. Later, he told the operator that some of the plane's passengers were planning to jump on the hijackers.

According to Jefferson, Beamer's last audible words were: "Are you guys ready? Let's roll."

Beamer's last words later became the war cry for those fighting al-Qaeda in Afghanistan.

In honor of the bravery of Beamer and others like him, a number of buildings now bear his name: a post office in Cranbury, New Jersey; a high school in Federal Way, Washington; and the student center on the campus of Wheaton (Illinois) College.

Widow Lisa Beamer poses for a photograph prior to signing copies of her new book *Let's Roll: Finding Hope in the Midst of Crisis* at Barnes & Noble, Westside Pavilion on August 21, 2002.

HEROES OF 9/11

Injured firefighter Armondo Reno is carried by fellow fire fighters away from the remains of the World Trade Center on September 11, 2001.

First Responders

On September 11, 2001, New York City suffered the most catastrophic terrorist attack ever to occur on American soil.

Thousands of civilian men, women and children were killed and many more were injured when two hijacked jetliners crashed into the World Trade Center.

The last, best hope for the community of people working in or near the Twin Towers that day rested not with policymakers but with first responders: fire, police, emergency medical service, and building safety professionals. These were the people who answered the alarms, ran toward danger and provided urgent care. They placed their own lives at risk in an attempt to save others.

More than 400 first responders were among that day's many victims. The New York City Fire Department alone lost 343 firefighters and paramedics that day. The New York City Police Department lost 23 officers; 37 Port Authority police officers were also killed.

New York City Police Officer Moria Smith was among the dead. Her bravery had been widely recognized prior to 9/11. She ran with the bulls in Spain. In 1991, she ran into a subway tunnel to rescue dozens of people trapped in one of the worst subway accidents in New York history.

On the morning of September 11, she ran toward danger once again, into the burning towers of the World Trade Center. A stock broker she helped to safety recalled her steady blue eyes and her even voice. The next day's papers carried an image of Moira helping an injured man out of the tower, before she rushed back in to save others. And then the tower collapsed around her.

One of Moira's colleagues said: "She could have saved herself, but nothing would have stopped her from saving one more person."

Timothy Stackpole, a 42-year-old father of five, was among the many firefighters who lost their lives that fateful day. Just days six days prior to the Trade Center attacks, Tim had been promoted to captain from lieutenant.

Tim's boss in the FDNY, Ed Van Vossen, said: "Timmy was just a wonderful, wonderful guy. He was about the best kind of guy you could ever hope to know."

A 20-year veteran of the FDNY, Tim had been badly burned in a 1998 fire but fought his way back to health to do the job he loved—a job he was performing when he perished on the morning of September 11.

Moira and Tim's stories are just two examples of the extraordinary bravery that took place that tragic day. Undeniably, those who risked their lives for others brought credit to the uniform, and honor to the United States of America.

US Soldiers from the 234th Infantry Division, Fort Riley, Kansas are seen inside of a plane to Afghanistan from the US transit center Manas 30kms from Bishkek on April 15, 2011.

Military Heroes

The victory over Osama bin Laden was borne heavily by our troops, intelligence officers and their families.

While much has been made of the U.S. Navy SEALs who actually carried out the attack on bin Laden, the truth is that more than 2 million American troops have deployed to Iraq and Afghanistan more than 3.3 million times since Sept. 11, 2001.

The Defense Department provides this break down by service:

Army: More than 1 million soldiers have deployed since the beginning of the wars. These 1 million soldiers have completed 1.5 million deployment events, with 352,700 deploying more than once.

Navy: More than 367,900 sailors have deployed since the beginning of the wars, with 147,200 deploying more than once. In all, the sailors have logged 595,700 deployments.

Marine Corps: More than 251,800 Marines have deployed since the start of the wars, completing 392,900 tours. More than 106,400 have deployed more than once.

Air Force: More than 389,900 airmen have deployed since 2001, with 185,500 going more than once. In all, airmen have completed 771,400 deployment events.

Coast Guard: More than 4,370 Coast Guardsmen have deployed since 2001, with 650 deploying more than once.

As of October 2010, the U.S. military reported 5,670 casualties in Operation Iraqi Freedom and Operation Enduring Freedom (Afghanistan).

"There are times where, in our country, we've got political disagreements. And appropriately we have big debates about war and peace," President Barack Obama told soldiers at Fort Bliss, in El Paso, Texas, on August 31, 2010.

"But the one thing we don't argue about is the fact that we've got the finest fighting force in the history of the world," the president said.

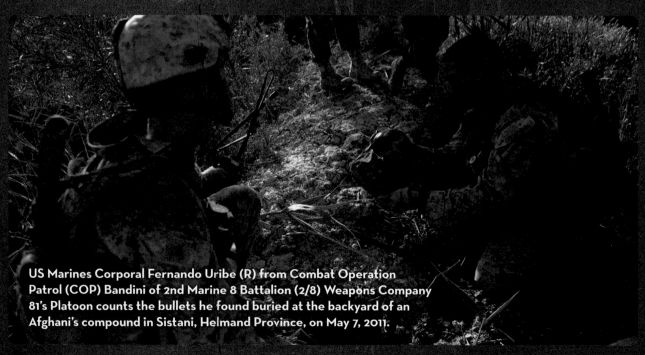

US Marines Corporal Fernando Uribe (R) from Combat Operation Patrol (COP) Bandini of 2nd Marine 8 Battalion (2/8) Weapons Company 81's Platoon counts the bullets he found buried at the backyard of an Afghani's compound in Sistani, Helmand Province, on May 7, 2011.

A T-shirt reading 'Osama Got Obama'd' is displayed at a souvenir stand near the White House in Washington on May 6, 2011, five days after al-Qaeda leader Osama bin Laden was killed by US Navy SEALs in Pakistan.

Navy SEALs Team 6

The elite team of Navy SEALs that carried out the assault on Osama bin Laden was stationed at Naval Air Station Oceana in Virginia Beach.

The United States Navy SEa, Air and Land (SEAL) Teams—commonly known as Navy SEALs—are a special operations force. The unit's acronym ("SEAL") is derived from their capacity to operate at sea, in the air, and on land – but it is their ability to work underwater that separates SEALs from most other military units in the world.

The SEALs' Team 6 is part of a counterterrorism group so specialized that no one can apply to join it. The operatives are recruited from existing SEAL teams. They are an elite group within the elite.

The team was formed in response to the 1980 American hostages rescue attempt in Iran. The effort failed and demonstrated the need for a counterterrorist team that could operate under the utmost secrecy.

Team 6 exists outside military protocol and engages in operations that are at the highest level of classification and often outside the boundaries of international law.

Team 6 has hunted down major al-Qaeda and Taliban figures since 2001, and also operated in Somalia, the former Yugoslavia, Afghanistan and Iraq.

Members are not allowed to talk about the elite group at all.

Members of Fighter Squadron 213 (Vf-213) squeeze another F-14 'Tomcat' into hangar 500 at naval air station Oceana, where SEALs Team 6 was stationed.

HEROES OF 9/11

US President George W. Bush speaks during a press conference in the Brady Press Briefing Room at the White House in Washington, DC, on January 12, 2009. President Bush mounted a defiant and emotional defense of his 'good, strong record,' rejecting criticism of his 'war on terror' tactics and policy in Iraq and on the economy.

Two presidents led the search for bin Laden

Terrorist Osama bin Laden was killed under President Barack Obama's watch. The search for him, though, started nearly 10 years ago, when President George W. Bush was in office. The current and former commanders in chief appeared willing to share the credit for his demise. Americans – specifically American politicians – were not so united in handing out thanks and praise.

President Obama claimed credit for himself when he took to the airwaves on the evening of May 1, 2011. He emphasized that the decision to make the bin Laden manhunt a key objective was his. He did not mention Bush, who shortly after the September 11, 2001, attacks declared he wanted bin Laden "dead or alive."

Shortly after bin Laden's death was announced, leading Republicans offered public praise for Obama's leadership. Additionally, a strong number of Republican voters in recent polls say they believe the president deserves credit for the mission's success.

US President Barack Obama announcing the death of Osama bin Laden at the White House in Washington DC, May 1, 2011.

But there's a stark divide between the parties when it comes to giving President Bush credit. A poll conducted by the Washington Post/Pew Research Center found that 81 percent of Republicans thought Bush deserved some recognition for the successful operation. Only 35 percent of Democrats agreed with that assessment.

Analysis conducted by the University of Minnesota similarly showed that credit for the successful mission was very much divided down party lines.

The University of Minnesota report found that 87 percent of Congressional representatives issued a press release on their official websites or made a statement about bin Laden via Facebook or Twitter. Analysis of those news releases reveled that:

- 60 percent of Democrats credited Obama or thanked him for his leadership, compared with 24 percent of Republicans who did the same.
- GOP House members were more likely to split the political credit between Obama and Bush.
- 20 percent of Republicans mentioned Bush in their statements, compared with 2.5 percent of Democrats who did.

The bickering over credit for success of the mission is likely to continue for years to come. However, while Americans may disagree over which president guided the most important part of the operation, it is clear that both presidents were instrumental in having bin Laden pay for his crimes against this country and others.

As New York grieved for its lost loved ones, hand made posters appeared all over Manhattan after the attacks on the World Trade Centre. New York. Picture shows a picture after the rain has caused much of the colours to run.

September 11, 2001 by the numbers

56 and 102	Number of minutes before the burning Twin Towers tumbled
2,996	Total number killed in attacks in New York, Washington D.C. and Pennsylvania
343	Number of firefighters and paramedics killed
23	Number of NYPD officers killed
37	Number of Port Authority police officers killed
60	Number of World Trade Center companies that lost people
36,000	Estimated units of blood donated to the New York Blood Center in response to the tragedy
20	Percentage of Americans who knew someone hurt or killed in the attacks
300	Number of firefighters on leave for respiratory problems resulting from the terrorist attacks
6	Days the New York Stock Exchange was closed following the attacks
684.81	Point drop in the Dow Jones industrial average when the NYSE reopened
146,100	Jobs lost in New York that were directly attributed to the attacks
26	Days after 9/11 before the United States began bombing Afghanistan
1.4 billion	Dollars donated to 9/11 charities
25	Percent of total charity money raised that went to FDNY and NYPD families

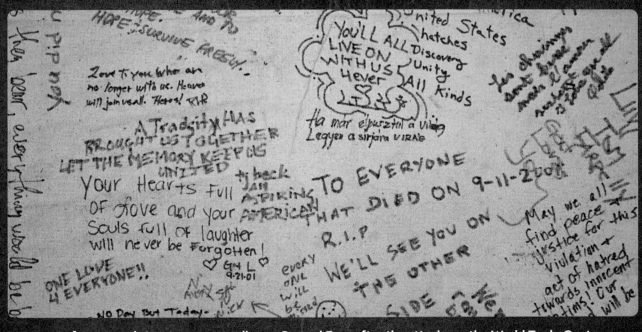

Messages of peace and signatures on a wall near Ground Zero after the attacks on the World Trade Center.

CHAPTER 2
OSAMA BIN LADEN AND AL-QAEDA

CHAPTER 2: **OSAMA BIN LADEN AND AL-QAEDA**

The first deployment of the Soviet army into Afghanistan began in December 1979. This military movement marked the beginning of a decade-long Soviet rule in the country. It also became a defining central government. This separation led to a revolt against the monarchy.

In April 1978, the Afghan communist party, the People's Democratic Party of Afghanistan, seized power in a coup and

Afghan anti-Soviet resistance fighters with their primitive arms in the eastern parts of the country. The Afghans repulsed the then Red Army 1979-1989 invasion with a huge human cost and with the material aid of the western world, above all, the United States.

struggle in Osama bin Laden's life.

After World War II, both the United States and Soviet Union competed for global power. After the United States established military ties with Pakistan in 1954, Afghanistan turned to the Soviet Union for support. In return, the Soviets used the strategic location of Afghanistan —between Asia and the Middle East—to counter the U.S.-Pakistan alliance.

When the Soviets entered Afghanistan, the country's monarchy was vulnerable. King Zahir Shah was unable to merge his nation's existing tribal society with a

killed the country's prime minister. This created an opportunity for a foreign invasion into a country that lacked a stable government leadership.

In 1978, Nur Mohammed Taraki became president of Afghanistan; Hafizullah Amin was named deputy prime minister.

Soon after seizing power, Taraki promoted the establishment of full women's rights and the implementation of land reform. The changes threatened Afghan traditions, and widespread resistance to them began in the summer of 1978. The reforms led to a power

The then Red Army invaded Afghanistan for 10 years only to suffer a humiliating defeat in the hands of the Afghan resistance groups backed by the west, above all the United States.

The Afghan western-backed Mujahideen resistance fighters man an anti-aircraft position in Kunar valley in the eastern province of Kunar on an unspecified date in the 80s.

Key Events Around the Soviet Invasion of Afghanistan

1978   Afghanistan's communist People's Democratic Party seizes power in a coup on April 27, but is split along ethnic lines and in-fighting begins. The country is renamed Democratic Republic of Afghanistan (DRA). An Islamic and conservative insurgency soon begins in the provinces.

1978   On December 5, a friendship treaty is signed with the USSR, building on Soviet economic and military support given to Afghanistan since the early 1950s.

1978   Prime Minister Mohammed Daoud Khan and his family are assassinated in the Saur Revolution and Nur Mohammad Taraki, leader of the People's Democratic Party of Afghanistan (PDPA), forms Afghanistan's first Marxist government. Babrak Karmal becomes deputy Prime Minister.

1979   In March, the USSR begins massive military aid to the DRA.

1979   President Nur Mohammed Taraki is killed in September and Hafizullah Amin emerges as DRA leader.

1979   On December 24, Soviet Commandos seize strategic installations in Kabul. Additional soldiers cross the border at Termez and Kushka heading toward Kabul and Herat respectively.

1979   On December 29, after a week of heavy fighting during which Soviet commandos kill Amin and tens of thousands of troops invade by ground and air, Babrak Kamal is installed as the DRA's new Soviet-backed leader.

1980   Resistance intensifies with Mujahideen groups fighting Soviet forces and their DRA allies. The United States, Pakistan and Saudi Arabia supply money and arms to the Mujahideen. The US leads a boycott of the Moscow Olympics.

1982   The United Nations General Assembly calls for Soviet withdrawal.

1985   More than 5 million Afghans are thought to have been displaced by the war, with many fleeing to neighboring Iran or Pakistan. Soviet leader Mikhail Gorbachev says he wants to end the war in Afghanistan. His escalation of troops leads to the bloodiest year of the war.

1986   The U.S. begins supplying the Mujahideen with Stinger missiles. Karmal is replaced by Mohammed Najibullah.

1988   The DRA, USSR, US and Pakistan sign peace accords and the Soviets begin pulling out troops.

1988   Bin Laden wants to continue the "holy war" beyond Afghanistan. Using the Services Office organization as a foundation, he forms al-Qaeda around 1988.

1989   On February 15, the USSR announces the departure of the last Soviet troops. Civil war continues as the Mujahideen push to overthrow Najibullah, who is eventually toppled in 1992.

struggle between Taraki and Amin and, ultimately, resulted in Taraki being killed by rebel groups in a palace shootout. Hafizullah Amin, Taraki's deputy prime minister, assumed power.

A guerrilla soldier aims a stinger missle at passing aircraft near a remote rebel base in the Safed Koh Mountains February 10, 1988 in Afghanistan.

and seized control of the capital.

Soviet troops then fanned out across Afghanistan to occupy major population centers, airbases and strategic lines of communication. The Soviets waged a full-fledged counter-insurgency campaign against the rebellious Muslim tribesmen who had been on the verge of winning a nearly two-year-long war against the Taraki-Amin communist regime. By late 1978, a rebellion against the Taraki government's policies started an Islamic extremist movement in eastern Afghanistan and spread throughout the country, leading to civil war.

Many Muslims regarded the struggle against the Soviets as a jihad. Muslims from around the world volunteered to fight with the Mujahideen. Osama bin Laden was one of the most notable of those volunteers.

On December 27, 1979, under the guise of an ongoing Soviet military buildup, heavily-armed Soviet soldiers were airlifted into Kabul, Afghanistan, to overthrow Amin's regime.

Shortly after the military operation began, Soviet troops overpowered presidential guards, captured Amin, executed him along with several members of his family for crimes against the people,

The young political activist traveled to the region, raised money from other wealthy Muslims to finance the fight and is said to have engaged in at least one battle himself. The war in Afghanistan lasted 10 years — basically the whole of the 1980s. John Parachini, an expert on

A guerrilla soldier sits holding artillery near a remote rebel base in the Safed Koh Mountains February 10, 1988 in Afghanistan. A Soviet-supported communist coup by the People's Democratic Party of Afghanistan led to the USSR's 1979 invasion of the Islamic nation, resulting in ten years of civil war between the Russian-led government and the US-backed Afghan rebels.

In Afghanistan between 1979 and 1989, during the Russian-Afghan war, Afghan Mujahideens—Muslims resisting Russian occupation—displayed their equipment against chemical warfare that they had stolen from Russian soldiers.

Bin Laden's Turning Point

1989. That was the year everything changed.

For the United States, which had supported the Afghan resistance with billions of dollars in arms and ammunition, the Soviet retreat in Afghanistan signaled the beginning of the end of the cold war.

For bin Laden, who had long supported the resistance, it was a sign that Muslim power was supreme and that he must continue to assert Islamic political power, toppling infidel governments through jihad.

Bin Laden was confident Muslims would put an end to America's reign as a superpower. By modeling himself after the Prophet Muhammad, he was preparing himself to become a player on the world stage.

The Prophet Muhammad, after all, had led the Muslim people in wars against nonbelievers from North Africa and the Middle East. Muhammad's work had been guided by the Quran Muhammad. Similarly, bin Laden saw his expulsions from Saudi Arabia and later from Sudan as signs that he, too, was a chosen one.

According to his visions, bin Laden would be a prince, building an empire that would begin in Afghanistan and then reach across the globe.

"These countries belong to Islam," he said in a 1998 interview, "not the rulers."

Al-Qaeda became the means of achieving his dream of world domination. Under this infrastructure, he created a web of businesses that could obtain and move all the weapons, chemicals and money he needed. He created training camps for foot soldiers, a media office to spread his word and set up councils to approve his military plans.

As the years passed, al-Qaeda grew. It developed relationships and partnerships with other terrorist groups. Bin Laden's cause was gaining momentum.

And it all started in 1989.

Osama bin Laden, the Saudi millionaire and fugitive leader of the terrorist group al Qaeda, explains why he has declared a 'jihad' or holy war against the United States on August 20, 1998.

Afghan national army all around Kabul, Afghanistan in February , 1989.

terrorism at the Rand Corp., said that for millions of Muslims and, very specifically for bin Laden, those years created a movement.

"In this period, there is an awakening throughout the Islamic world about fighting a great struggle—beyond the struggle that many fundamentalist Islamic groups were fighting in their own nations," Parachini told NPR.

Al-Qaeda grew out of the Services Office, a clearinghouse for the international Muslim brigade opposed to the 1979 Soviet invasion of Afghanistan. Bin Laden and the Palestinian religious scholar Abdullah Azzam ran the Services Office in the 1980s. Bin Laden set up a financial support network known as the "Golden Chain," comprised mainly of financiers from Saudi Arabia and Persian Gulf states. Using this immense new fund, the group recruited, trained, and financed thousands of foreign Mujahideen (holy warriors) from more than fifty countries.

Bin Laden wanted these fighters to continue the "holy war" beyond Afghanistan. Using the Services Office organization as a foundation, he formed al-Qaeda around 1988.

In 1989, when the Soviets withdrew from Afghanistan, bin Laden went home

Members of an Afghan Mujahideen group during a lull in an advance on Jalalabad, Afghanistan, March 1989.

Arab militant Osama bin Laden poses for this undated photo.

Evil Charisma

How does someone convince someone to murder on his behalf? To strap bombs to their bodies? To fly suicide missions?

Osama bin Laden unquestionably had the capacity to convince others to undertake some gruesome tasks. But how?

"I viewed him as a charismatic figure," former New Jersey Gov. Tom Kean, who was co-chairman of the 9/11 commission, said in an interview with New Jersey Network.

"People come along sometime who can move crowds, who by their personality can attract other people to a movement. That's what he did," he said.

Kean described bin Laden as equal parts mad genius and religion zealot.

Mark Stern, professor emeritus of Iona College in New York and an expert in the psychology of evil and Messianic figures, believes bin Laden was different from other evil charismatics, such as Adolph Hitler, mass murderer Charles Manson and Jim Jones, leader of the People's Temple.

"He had more of a political world view—more like a desire to save the world than to destroy it and rebuild it in his image," said Stern.

Bin Laden had somehow amassed mesmerizing power over his followers. He had a plan he believed in and he convinced others they should not only support that plan, but be willing to die for it.

"We live in a world of social and psychological influence," said Steve Hassan, founder of the Boston-based organization Freedom of Mind and an expert on brainwashing. "Agents of influence are effective at what they do. But some people come along who have a personality type and are often described as narcissistic."

In a paper presented at the 2002 Annual Scientific Meeting of the International Society of Political Psychology, researcher Aubrey Immelman said bin Laden's blend of Ambitious and Dauntless personality patterns suggests the presence of Millon's "unprincipled narcissist."

This composite combines the narcissist's arrogant sense of self-worth, exploitative indifference to the welfare of others, and grandiose expectation of special recognition with a disregard for the rights of others.

Immelman went on to say bin Laden did not fit the profile of the closed-minded religious fundamentalist, nor that of the religious martyr who is generally self-sacrificing. Rather, his analysis suggests bin Laden was adept at exploiting Islamic fundamentalism in the service of his own ambition and personal dreams of glory.

A video grab of Osama bin Laden's al-Qaeda.

to Saudi Arabia. But his relations with the country's leaders soon soured. Saudi Arabian leaders revoked bin Laden's passport and, later, his citizenship.

This man without a country spent the

A video grab dated June 19, 2001, shows Saudi dissident Osama bin Laden firing an AK-47 (Kalashnikov) sub-machine-gun in a video tape said to have been prepared and released by bin Laden himself.

next five years in exile in Sudan. Terrorism scholar John Parachini said those years—from 1991 to 1996—were a critical time.

"Here is where the modern-day bin Laden really comes to the front, because it's he, with his considerable wealth, operating in a weak state," Parachini said. "So here you have this confluence of interest of a newly emerged Islamic state, and a newly emerged, subnational, loosely

affiliated collection of people that we now know as al-Qaeda."

Al-Qaeda has since grown into an international terrorist network. It is considered the top terrorist threat to the United States. The group is wanted for its September 11, 2001, attacks on the World Trade Center and the Pentagon, as well as a host of lesser attacks. Al-Qaeda has no single headquarters. From 1991 to 1996, al-Qaeda operated out of Pakistan, primarily along the Afghan border. During the Taliban's reign, al-Qaeda shifted its base of operations into Afghanistan.

Analysts believe al-Qaeda is training or has trained most of the terrorist groups in Pakistan's tribal areas. It has introduced its practice of suicide bombings to both the Afghan and the Pakistani Taliban, as well as affiliated groups in Iraq, Yemen, and North Africa.

Officials say al-Qaeda has underground cells in some 100 countries. Law enforcement has broken up al-Qaeda cells in the United Kingdom, United States, Italy, France, Spain, Germany, Albania, Uganda, and elsewhere.

Pakistani protesters offer evening prayer during one of the biggest protest rallies against a possible U.S.-led war with Iraq March 2, 2003 in Karachi, Pakistan. At least 100,000 Islamic party activists attended the march. The six Islamic parties alliance Muttahida Majlis-e-Amal (MMA), which had vowed to bring one million people on the streets, claimed half a million had already gathered. People carrying MMA flags and portraits of Osama bin Laden chanted 'Jihad (holy war)' and 'No blood for oil.'

What is Jihad?

"Jihad," particularly as used by Western media, is often defined as a holy war between followers of different religions.

More conventionally, Al-Hajj Talib 'Abdur-Rashid, imam of New York's Mosque of Islamic Brotherhood, says the word jihad refers to three different "levels" of struggle—personal, verbal and physical.

A *personal jihad*, called the Jihadun-Nafs, is the struggle to rid one's soul of evil influences. It is the inner battle to cleanse one's spirit of sin.

Muhammad encouraged Muslims to demand justice in the name of Allah via a *verbal jihad*. This action calls for followers to strive for justice through words and non-violent actions.

A *physical jihad* refers to the use of physical force in defense of Muslims against oppression and transgression by the enemies of Allah, Islam and Muslims. Allah commands that Muslims lead peaceful lives. If they are persecuted and oppressed, the Quran recommends that they migrate to a more peaceful land. If relocation isn't possible, Allah requires Muslims to defend themselves against oppression by "fighting against those who fight against us." The Quran states: "To those against whom war is made, permission is given [to defend themselves], because they are wronged – and verily, Allah is Most Powerful to give them victory."

أخطـر رجـل فى العـالـم شـاب
عمره ٤١ سنة وثروتة ٣٠٠ مليون دولار

A Palestinian militant from the Islamic Jihad movement displays a portrait of Saudi dissident Osama bin Laden.

Al-Qaeda was established by Osama bin Laden, Ayman Muhammad Rabaie al-Zawahiri and Jamal Ahmed Mohamed al-Fadl in Peshawar, Pakistan, around 1988. In building al-Qaeda, the trio meshed

The al-Qaeda network's alleged number two, Ayman al-Zawahri.

رسالة صوتية لأيمن الظواهري / الرجل الثاني في تنظيم القاعدة

رسالة صوتية مسجلة لأيمن الظواهري
الرجل الثاني في تنظيم القاعدة

their extraordinary Saudi wealth, the expertise of a lifetime Egyptian militant, and a philosophical foundation for jihad from a Cairo intellectual.

The organization was designed to help finance, recruit, transport and train thousands of fighters from dozens of countries to be part of an Afghan resistance to defeat the Soviet Union. But it didn't stop there.

Al-Qaeda continues to fight to establish a pan-Islamic Caliphate throughout the world, working with other Islamic extremist groups to overthrow regimes

it deems "non-Islamic" and expelling Westerners and non-Muslims from Muslim countries.

Messages articulated by bin Laden and others have inspired al-Qaeda members to take up arms. In short, bin Laden's message asserts that the West represents a threat to Islam; that loyalty to religion and loyalty to democratic institutions and values are incompatible; and that violence is the only proper response.

Al-Qaeda opposes Western influences and ideas that it regards as "unIslamic." It is explicitly opposed to democratic principles. It has released statements rejecting democratic elections in Iraq, Afghanistan and the Palestinian Territories. It claims democracy is a rival "religion" and that principles such as freedom of speech and freedom of religion are equivalent to apostasy, punishable by death.

Following the Soviet Union's withdrawal from Afghanistan in February 1989, bin Laden returned to his homeland, where he was hailed as a hero of jihad.

However, the Iraqi invasion of Kuwait in 1990 and Saddam Hussein's pan-Arab ideology suddenly put the Saudi monarchy at risk. Bin Laden offered King

Undated file picture of the head of the al-Qaeda terror network Osama bin Laden at an undisclosed place inside Afghanistan.

U.S. marines conduct a cordon and search raid at a suspected al-Qaeda hide-out January 1, 2002, in Afghanistan.

What does 'al-Qaeda' mean?

Al-Qaeda's leadership has always maintained the importance of having a "safe haven."

The very words *al-Qaeda* mean "the base" in Arabic.

In a 2001 interview with Arabic-language news network Al Jazeera, bin Laden explained the name is not a reference to a figurative foundation but, rather, to a physical spot for training.

"Abu Ubaidah Al Banjshiri (an early military commander of al-Qaeda) created a military base to train the young men to fight. ... So this place was called 'The Base,' as in a training base, and the name grew from this," he said.

It quickly became clear, though, that when al-Qaeda leadership said it wanted a "base," it actually meant it wanted a "state."

Shortly after the September 11 terrorist attacks, al-Qaeda higher-up Ayman Muhammad Rabaie al-Zawahiri released his autobiography, in which he explained:

"Confronting the enemies of Islam, and launching jihad against them require a Muslim authority, established on a Muslim land that raises the banner of jihad and rallies the Muslims around it. Without achieving this goal our actions will mean nothing."

A video grab dated June 19, 2001, shows members of Saudi dissident Osama bin Laden's al-Qaeda—or 'the base'—organization.

Fahd his Mujahideen fighters to defend the kingdom, warning him not to depend on non-Muslim troops for protection. Bin Laden believed the presence of foreign troops in the "land of the two mosques"

Over 1,000 US Marines from Fort Bragg disembark 21 August 1990 from a Galaxy transport plane at Saudi Dhahran air base.

(Mecca and Medina) dirtied sacred soil.

When King Fahd allowed the United States to station 300,000 troops on Saudi soil in preparation for the first Gulf War, bin Laden turned against the monarchy and fled into exile in Sudan.

Many believe that bin Laden's first bombing with al-Qaeda came in late 1992, when the Gold Mihor Hotel in Aden was bombed, killing two people. Bin Laden then went on to fund many jihadis in Algeria, Egypt, and Afghanistan throughout the 1990s. In 1998, bin Laden organized a series of bombings on U.S.

Embassy buildings in Dar es Salaam, Tanzania, and Nairobi; hundreds of people were killed in these bombings. This was a significant turning point in U.S. history because it was first time that bin Laden and al-Qaeda were truly brought to the American public's attention.

In 1996, bin Laden returned to Afghanistan, where he developed a close relationship with Mullah Omar, the leader of the new Taliban government.

As bin Laden presided over al-Qaeda's rise in the 1990s and early 2000s, the group's death count grew. The group took credit for massacres and bombings in Egypt, Kenya, Tanzania, and aboard a U.S. Naval ship.

In February 1996, bin Laden issued a fatwa declaring all American citizens legitimate targets of al-Qaeda and calling for Muslims to fulfill their duty by killing them. His message, in part, said:

"We—with God's help—call on every Muslim who believes in God and wishes to be rewarded to comply with God's order to kill the Americans and plunder their money wherever and whenever they find it. We also call on Muslim ulema,

A US Apache attack helicopter carrying Hellfire missiles over the Saudi desert before the allied intervention in Kuwait during the Persian Gulf War, December 1990.

Two F-117A aircraft from the 37th Tactical Fighter Wing (37th TFW) sit in a hangar during Operation Desert Shield.

The War on Terror

The United States' dedication to the "War on Terror" is long lived, but the actual phrase (or at least similar phrases) weren't used until about 27 years ago.

In 1984, the Reagan Administration used the term "War Against Terrorism" in its campaign to pass legislation designed to freeze the assets of terrorist organizations.

The exact phrase "War on Terror" was first used by U.S. President George W. Bush to denote a global military, political, legal and ideological struggle against terrorist organizations and regimes that were accused of having a connection to them or providing them with support.

On September 16, 2001, at Camp David, President George W. Bush said:

"This crusade—this war on terrorism—is going to take a while. ... And the American people must be patient. I'm going to be patient. But I can assure the American people, I am determined."

Four days later, during a televised address to a joint session of congress, Bush launched the war on terror when he said:

"Our 'War on Terror' begins with al-Qaeda, but it does not end there. It will not end until every terrorist group of global reach has been found, stopped and defeated."

The administration of U.S. President Barack Obama does not officially use the phrase "War on Terror." In fact, in 2009, the Defense Department changed the name of the country's anti-terrorism operation from "Global War on Terror" to "Overseas Contingency Operation."

Different name, same basic mission.

Two Marines wearing M-17A1 field protective masks man a fighting position on the perimeter of their camp while taking part in a training exercise during Operation Desert Shield.

Afghan men sit under guard at a traffic checkpoint conducted by the U.S. Army July 1, 2003, on the outskirts of Kandahar, Afghanistan. The U.S Army conducts random checkpoints as they contiune to search for Taliban and al-Qaeda suspects, weapons, and drugs.

leaders, youths, and soldiers to launch the raid on Satan's U.S. troops and the devil's supporters allying with them, and to displace those who are behind them so that they may learn a lesson."

Throughout much of the 1990s, al-Qaeda didn't so much recruit new members as it acquired them. The group systematically absorbed regional jihadist organizations, both venerable and newly created, and convinced them that their struggles were a component of al-Qaeda's sweeping international agenda. Over the years, al-Qaeda merged with groups including the Salafist Group for Preaching and Combat and Egyptian Islamic Jihad. Meanwhile, militant groups like al Shabaab, Al-Gama'a al-Islamiyya, Jamaat Islamiyya, and the Libyan Islamic Fighting Group have chosen not to merge but instead partner with al-Qaeda.

Because of the decentralized structure of the organization, it's impossible to know precisely how large al-Qaeda is. It is believed that the organization trained more than 5,000 militants in camps in

United States Army 10th Mountain soldiers take over a dwelling March 8, 2002, near the villages of Sherkhankheyl, Marzak, and Bobelkiel, Afghanistan. The villages were an al-Qaeda and Taliban stronghold, which came under intense bombing and firefights as the coalition forces battled to root them out.

Islamic Scholar and spiritual leader Shaykh-ul-Islam Dr Muhammad Tahir-ul Qadri delivers a terrorism Fatwa at the Institution of Mechanical Engineers on March 2, 2010, in London, England.

What is a Fatwa?

A fatwa is an Islamic religious decree or scholarly opinion on a matter of Islamic law.

Any recognized religious authority in Islam may issue a fatwa. Because there is no hierarchical priesthood in Islam, a fatwa is not considered "binding." Anyone who issues a fatwa is supposed to be knowledgeable and base their fatwas in both knowledge and wisdom. The decrees are to cite evidence from Islamic sources. Because fatwas are based on opinion, it is not uncommon for different scholars to reach—and share—different conclusions on the same issue.

Muslims are advised to consider the fatwa, the reputation of the person issuing the fatwa, and the evidence provided in support of it. Then, they can decide whether or not to follow that fatwa.

One of bin Laden's most noted fatwas was issued in 1996 and then re-released, in a shorter version, in 1998. The fatwa, in part, reads:

"We—with God's help—call on every Muslim who believes in God and wishes to be rewarded to comply with God's order to kill the Americans and plunder their money wherever and whenever they find it. We also call on Muslim ulema, leaders, youths, and soldiers to launch the raid on Satan's U.S. troops and the devil's supporters allying with them, and to displace those who are behind them so that they may learn a lesson."

Muhammad Tahir-ul-Qadri, a Pakistan born Islamic scholar, made headlines of his own in 2010 when he issued a fatwa condemning terrorism and suicide bombings. The fatwa, issued at a press conference in London, very directly challenged al-Qaeda's "violent ideology."

Police wait outside Stockwell Underground Station in London, July 22, 2005, following the shooting of a suspected suicide bomber.

Afghanistan since the late 1980s. Today, much of al-Qaeda's recruitment is done online. In early 2011, a prominent Saudi scholar went public with his plea to parents, imams of mosques and schools to be vigilant regarding children's Internet usage.

Al-Qaeda leaders have conducted sophisticated public relations and media campaigns since the mid-1990s. Terrorism analysts believe these campaigns have been designed to elicit psychological reactions and communicate complex political messages to a global audience as well as to specific populations in the Islamic world, the United States, Europe, and Asia.

Al-Qaeda's *Inspire* magazine, for example, is an English version of *Jihadi* magazine designed for the Western world. The cosmopolitan-looking publication covers a wide variety of subjects from jihad to exercising in the field. Every issue has a "how-to" that explains the basics of things like bomb-making or tossing a grenade. The magazine's fifth issue was released in April 2011.

Some officials and analysts believe there is more to al-Qaeda's messages than first meets the eye. It is suspected that the

Pedestrians walk along the Embankment after terrorist attacks in London severly reduced bus service and closed the Underground on July 7, 2005.

A picture taken on September 11, 2008, shows Omar bin Laden, the fourth son of Osama bin Laden, during a dinner that he and his English wife Zaina hosted at their horse ranch, at the foot of Abu Sir pyramids on the outskirts of Cairo. One of al-Qaeda founder Osama bin Laden's sons has asked for political asylum in Spain, an interior ministry spokesman said on November 4, 2008, confirming a report in top-selling daily newspaper *El Pais*.

No al-Qaeda for Osama's sons?

In what is believed to be the last will and testament of Osama bin Laden, the terrorist allegedly apologizes to his children for devoting his life to jihad and tells them not to join al-Qaeda.

The document was first published in a Lebanese newspaper in 2001. It has resurfaced several times and became the subject of much speculation immediately following the May 1, 2011 death of bin Laden at the hands of U.S. soldiers.

Despite the document's ubiquity, U.S. intelligence sources say they are skeptical of its authenticity.

In the document, bin Laden apologizes to his children for spending so much time devoted to jihad. He tells them not work for al Qaeda. He compares himself to a seventh century caliph and suggests if they want to climb the ranks of the terror network, they must do so by their own murderous deeds and not by riding his bloody coattails.

"As for you my children: Forgive me for not giving you except but a minimum amount of my time since I have begun my call for jihad," the document, allegedly penned by bin Laden, says. "And I advise you not to join in the work of al-Qaeda."

Rohan Gunaratna, head of the International Centre for Political Violence and Terrorism Research, believes bin Laden's reluctance to guarantee his sons a leadership role in al-Qaeda is proof that the document is authentic.

"I have no doubt this document is real," he said. "Despite being puritanical, bin Laden had a rather modern management style."

Bin Laden's own sons doubt the document is genuine, saying their father was grooming them to take over al-Qaeda.

"He never asked me to join al-Qaeda, but he did tell me I was the son chosen to carry on his work," Omar bin Laden, Osama's son, told the *Guardian* in 2009.

Additionally, the purported will insists that bin Laden's wives not remarry after his death, instead devoting their time and energy to "care for our children and sacrifice for them and make prayers for them."

The document is dated December 14, 2001. Terrorism expert Gunaratna said the signature at the bottom of the document belonged to bin Laden. Additionally, a 2009 report released by the United States Senate Committee on Foreign Relations says the will is "regarded as authentic." That report does not indicate how the document was authenticated.

Pakistani photographer Mazhar Khan displays his photographs of Osama bin Laden's son taken in Afghanistan, before giving a press conference in Islamabad on May 4, 2011.

Policemen accompany an alleged member of al-Qaeda from the Federal High Court of Justice to a helicopter on April 30, 2011, in Karlsruhe, southern Germany. One of three alleged members of al-Qaeda detained in Germany was ordered by a high-ranking member of the group in the year 2010 to carry out an attack in the country.

phenomenon. It changes continuously," Dr. Bruce Hoffman, terror expert and Georgetown University professor said in 2006.

"Even before 9/11, al-Qaeda was not a monolithic organization. Certainly today it is not the same as it was on 9/11. It doesn't have a state within a state anymore, as it had in Afghanistan. It doesn't have a network of training camps and operational bases and a very solid command-and-control nexus. But now a lot of those training capabilities have migrated from physical space to virtual space, because the terrorists are using the Internet much more ... I think that al-Qaeda still exercises command-and-control. The attacks on the London Underground in July 2005 show that. And there are indications that the recently unmasked London airliner plot from this summer will, too. Al-Qaeda is still alive and kicking and, as the airliner plot may yet show, still thinking in the same grandiose, ambitious terms as before 9/11," he said.

printed and taped messages often contain signals that instruct operatives to prepare for and carry out new attacks.

Terrorism experts have widely differing opinions about the strength and vitality of a current-day al-Qaeda. Some believe bin Laden's death will weaken the organization. Others say bin Laden has been in hiding and out of a key leadership role for years, so his death won't have much of an affect. Still others fear the U.S. killing of bin Laden will galvanize terrorists against the United States.

"You must look at terror as a constant

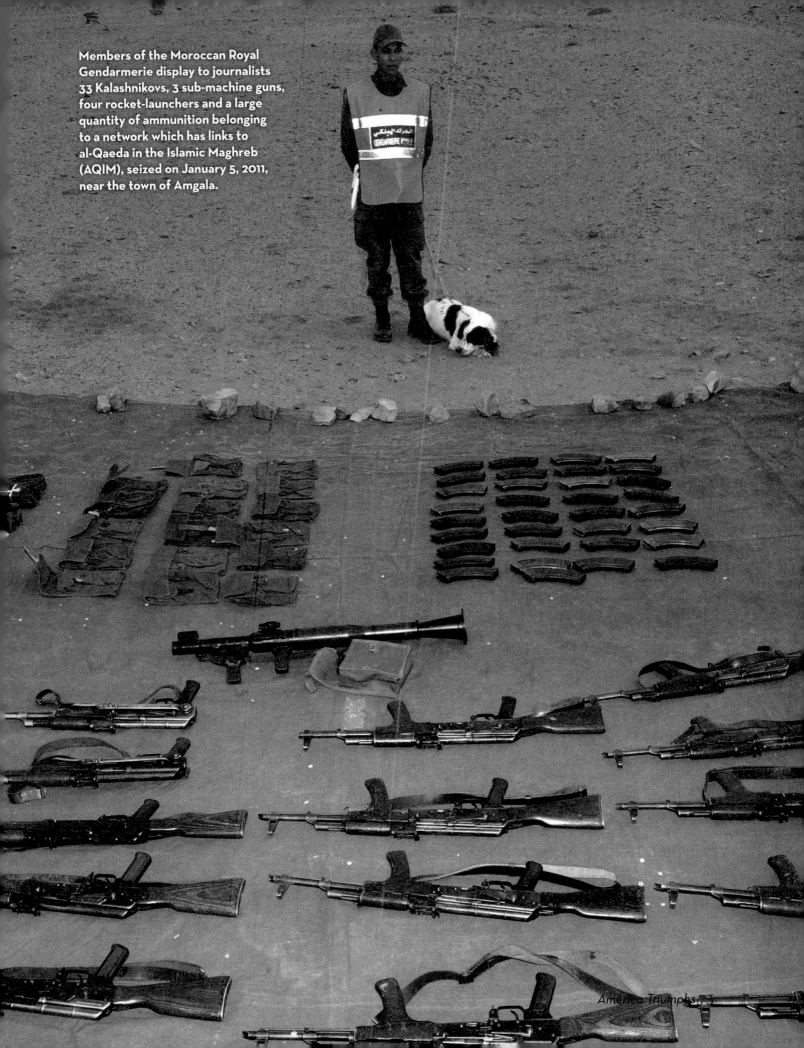

Members of the Moroccan Royal Gendarmerie display to journalists 33 Kalashnikovs, 3 sub-machine guns, four rocket-launchers and a large quantity of ammunition belonging to a network which has links to al-Qaeda in the Islamic Maghreb (AQIM), seized on January 5, 2011, near the town of Amgala.

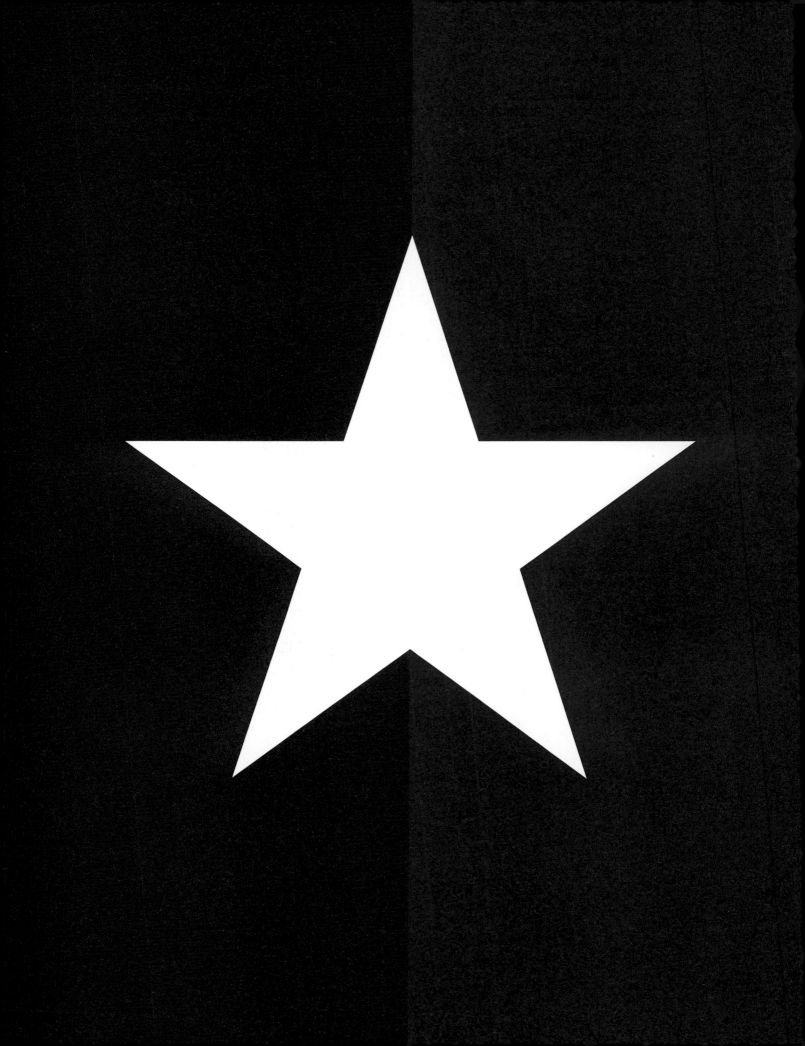

CHAPTER 3
HUNTING A TERRORIST

In 2006, U.S. operatives searching for Osama bin Laden admitted it had been two long years since they had received a credible lead about the terrorist's whereabouts.

"The handful of assets we have, have given us nothing close to real-time

problem was that no one knew where the "zone" was.

"Here you've got a guy who's gone off the net and is hiding in some of the most formidable terrain in one of the most remote parts of the world surrounded by people he trusts implicitly," T.

intelligence" said one counterterrorism official, who said the trail, despite the most extensive manhunt in U.S. history, had gone "stone cold."

Frustrated by the futile hunt, President George W. Bush issued a mid-2006 order to "flood the zone"—sharply increasing the number of intelligence offers and assets dedicated to the search. As welcome as the additional resources were, counterterrorism officials said the

McCreary, spokesman for the National Counterterrorism Center, told the *New York Times*. "And he stays off the net and is probably not mobile. That's an extremely difficult problem."

U.S. officials had a hunch that bin Laden was hiding in the northern portion of a remote and relatively wild tribal region along the Afghanistan-Pakistan border. Lack of activity elsewhere and a videotape that showed bin Laden walking

US Army soldiers from 2-506 Infantry 101st Airborne Division and Afghan National Policemen and Army load onto a UH-47 Chinook helicopter landing to pick them up during day three of Operation Shir Pacha into the Derezda Valley in the rugged Spira mountains in Khost province, along the Afghan-Pakistan border.

Jim Rydbom / Associated Press

Civilian Searches for Osama

When Osama bin Laden disparaged both God and the United States of America, Gary Brooks Faulkner decided he needed to take matters into his own hands.

The construction worker from Greeley, Colorado, sold his belongings and launched his own search for bin Laden.

Faulkner made headlines around the world in June 2010, after he was detained nine miles from the Afghanistan border by Pakistani police. A devout Christian, Faulkner said he was on a mission from God to lop off bin Laden's head with a samurai sword. In addition to a 40-inch sword, the ex-con was armed with a pistol,

al-Qaeda leader.

"My brother is not crazy. He is highly intelligent and loves his country and he has not forgotten what Osama has done to this country," Scott Faulkner told CNN.

Upon hearing that bin Laden had been killed by U.S. Navy SEALs, Gary Brooks Faulkner claimed partial credit, saying he had flushed the terrorist out of his cave and into the compound where he was found. He said he deserves a portion of the $27 million reward for serving up bin Laden "on a platter."

"I scared the squirrel out of his hole, he popped his head up and he got capped," Faulkner told ABC News. "They were

FBI TEN MOST WANTED FUGITIVE

MURDER OF U.S. NATIONALS OUTSIDE THE UNITED STATES; CONSPIRACY TO MURDER U.S. NATIONALS OUTSIDE THE UNITED STATES; ATTACK ON A FEDERAL FACILITY RESULTING IN DEATH

USAMA BIN LADEN

Date of Photograph Unknown

REWARD
Up to $10,000,000 USD
ABU MUSAB AL ZARQAWI

This man is wanted for murdering innocent women and children.

carrying night goggles, some Christian texts and a small amount of hashish. The Pakistanis decided Faulkner was not a threat and sent him packing.

Scott Faulkner called his brother, Gary, a "bulldog" who was determined to find the

handed this opportunity on a platter from myself. I wanted to bring him to justice. I'm not greedy, but I sold everything I had and I put my life on the line."

The State Department had no immediate comment on Faulkner's claims.

US Marines Corporal Joshua Boston (L) from Combat
Operation Patrol (COP) Bandini of 2nd Marine
8 Batallion (2/8) Weapons Company 81's Platoon
interogates an Afghani youth.

on a trail toward Pakistan at the end of the battle of Tora Bora in December 2001, were two of the most viable clues in hand.

For years, the search kept coming up empty. The CIA didn't have access to people close to al-Qaeda's inner circle. Pakistan officials were unwilling to help in the search. The Taliban and al-Qaeda reemerged in Afghanistan. The Iraqi insurgence put demands on U.S. military and intelligence resources.

Bin Laden had been so elusive for so long, that some U.S. operatives began referring to him as "Elvis," in recognition of wishful-thinking sightings that never turned out to be valid.

During years of painstaking intelligence work, dozens of CIA detainees were interrogated in prisons in Eastern Europe. Intelligence agencies eavesdropped on telephone calls. They read thousands of intercepted e-mails. They studied satellite images of the area.

Then, in July 2010, Pakistanis working for the U.S. Central Intelligence Agency saw a white Suzuki driving through the busy streets of Peshawar, Pakistan. They wrote down the car's license plate. What seemed like just another long shot turned into the key in the search for bin Laden.

The man in that car was bin Laden's most trusted courier. CIA operatives spent the next month tracking him through central Pakistan. Finally, he led them to a large compound at the end of a long dirt road. The compound was surrounded by tall security fences in an affluent village about 35 miles from Peshawar,

Intelligence officers monitored the compound for months. They watched who went in and who came out. They recorded dates and times of activity.

Then, on May 1, 2011, 79 American commandos in four helicopters

US Marines Lance Corporal Michael Horne from Combat Operation Patrol (COP) Bandini of 2nd Marine 8 Batallion (2/8) Weapons Company 81's Platoon gets ready to open fire in Sistani, Helmand Province, on May 7, 2011.

descended on the compound. Shots rang out. One of the U.S. helicopters stalled and would not take off. Pakistani authorities, kept in the dark by their allies in Washington, scrambled forces as the

US President Barack Obama and Vice President Joe Biden shake hands with Commander of US Special Operations Command (USSOCOM) Admiral Eric Olson as he arrives at Fort Campbell, Kentucky, May 6, 2011, where he is to meet with SEAL Team 6 and speak to soldiers from the 101st Airborne Division.

Mission Details Clarified Over Time

Within just a few days of the killing of Osama bin Laden, U.S. officials backed away from several details concerning its initial account of the mission.

On May 2, 2011, the day after the attack, John Brennan, a counterterrorism adviser to Barack Obama, said bin Laden was "engaged in a firefight" with his assailants and he did not know if he "got off any rounds." Other U.S. officials said bin Laden had actually fired at members of the U.S. Navy's SEAL Team 6.

Two days later, however, U.S. officials suggested that, when confronted at the high-security complex, bin Laden resisted but did not have a weapon and did not fire at his assailants.

Additionally, reporters were initially told that one of bin Laden's wives was killed while he was using her as a human shield. The news prompted headlines such as "Osama bin Laden Killed Cowering Behind his 'Human Shield' Wife" and "U.S.: Osama Used Wife as Human Shield."

Within a day, U.S. officials clarified that bin Laden's wife was shot in the calf and did not die in the assault, although another woman was killed.

"Two women were shot here," said a U.S. government official. "It sounds like their fates were mixed up. This is hours old and the full facts are still being ascertained as those involved are debriefed."

Initial reports of the attack indicated that bin Laden's son Hamza was killed alongside his father.

Obama staffer Brennan later amended that report to say it was bin Laden's son Khalid—not Hamza—who was killed.

Brennan said the misinformation about the assault came about because he and others had to garner information from live video feeds of the raid.

"I wasn't there," he said.

Pakistani policemen stand guard outside the hideout house of slain al-Qaeda leader Osama bin Laden in Abbottabad on May 5, 2011. US officials said they gave no notice to Pakistan before the May 2, 2011 daring raid, in which special forces killed the world's most wanted man at a mansion near the country's top military academy in Abbottabad.

CHAPTER 3: **HUNTING A TERRORIST**

American commandos rushed to finish their mission.

As the helicopters flew over Pakistani territory, President Barack Obama and his advisers gathered in the Situation Room of the White House to monitor the operation. Silence filled the air. President

man; he'd been shot in the head. One of the Navy SEALs on the mission snapped his photograph and uploaded it to analysts who fed it into a facial recognition program.

The SEALs searched the house floor by floor, room by room. As they climbed

President Barack Obama and Vice President Joe Biden, along with with members of the national security team, receive an update on the mission against Osama bin Laden in the Situation Room of the White House in Washington, D.C., May 1, 2011.

Obama looked "stone faced," an aide said. Vice President Joseph R. Biden Jr. fingered his rosary beads. Secretary of State Hillary Rodham Clinton sat with her hand over her face.

"The minutes passed like days," recalled John O. Brennan, the White House counterterrorism chief, who sat in the room with the president.

The mission was successful.

One of the five victims was a bearded

to the top floor, bin Laden's son came onto the stairs, brandishing a weapon. They took him down. As they entered the bedroom, bin Laden's wife rushed at them. She was shot in the leg. And then they found, shot and killed bin Laden himself.

"Geronimo," one of the SEALs reported, using the code name assigned to the world's most wanted terrorist. Shots were fired. "Geronimo EKIA," was the report from U.S. Military personnel. Enemy killed

Pakistanis along with international and local media gather outside Osama bin Laden's compound, where he was killed during a raid by U.S. special forces, May 3, 2011, in Abottabad, Pakistan.

A reader points to a death notice for Osama bin Laden placed in News Limited's *Daily Telegraph* newspaper in Sydney on May 3, 2011.

DEATH NOTICE

BIN LADEN, Osama
late of Pakistan
Passed away May 2, 2011

Devoted father of terrorism, genocidal mastermind, despised by all who loved peace and freedom. Lamented friend of oppression, hatred and horror. Will be sadly missed by al-Qaeda's mass murderers and Taliban terrorists. **A celebration mass will be held across the free world**

in action.

The SEALs were in and out of the compound in 40 minutes. Those 40 minutes ended history's most expensive and exasperating manhunt.

At 1:15 a.m. the morning of May 2 in Pakistan, the lifeless body of the world's most feared terrorist was placed in a helicopter for burial at sea, never to be seen or feared again. A nation that suffered its worst terrorist attack at his hands breathed a collective sigh. The mastermind behind 9/11 was dead at last.

In a rare Sunday night address from the East Room of the White House, President Obama announced that a small team of U.S. personnel attacked a compound in Pakistan's Abbottabad Valley, where bin Laden had been hiding.

"The United States has conducted an operation that has killed Osama bin Laden, the leader of al-Qaeda and a terrorist who's responsible for the deaths of thousands of innocent men, women and children," said Obama in his address to the nation. "A small team of Americans carried out with the operation with extraordinary courage and capability. After a firefight, they killed Osama bin Laden, and took custody of his body."

Upon hearing the news, America erupted in celebration.

The news dominated the Twitter real-time text feed. Spontaneous demonstrations by thousands of exultant Americans took place, most notably outside the White House and at Ground Zero in New York City. College students painted their faces red, white and blue; families waved flags; and fire fighters pumped their fists in the air. Crowds of strangers sang the national anthem.

"I felt I just needed to be here," Nancy Palo told *USA Today*. She lit two candles

at Ground Zero to commemorate the lost World Trade Center towers. "I feel bittersweet. It's an exciting time, but it's also a time to remember, a time to look forward but also a time to never forget."

Capture leads to Clean-Shaven Chin

Gary Weddle, a Middle School teacher in the tiny town of Ephrata, Washington, was deeply affected by the terrorist attacks of September 11, 2001.

He remembers staring at his television set, watching images that etched themselves into his mind. He wanted to do something to support the United States Military and American freedoms. He wanted to make a statement—and that's what he did ... with his beard.

At first, Weddle was so caught up in the news that he neglected to shave. A week or so later, he vowed not to shave until bin Laden was captured or proven dead. He figured it would just be a month or two. So his beard grew. And grew. And grew.

For almost 10 years, his beard grew, providing almost daily opportunities for Weddle to talk with students or strangers in the store or friends around the corner about what it meant to take a stand for something you believe in. Each year, the 50-year-old teacher explained to his students his beard was a reminder of the attacks on September 11, 2001.

Weddle has wanted to cut his beard for years. His wife, Donita, has wanted him to cut it, too. But for Weddle a vow is a vow, and so he hadn't even trimmed his long, bushy facial hair.

Then, 3,454 days after that 2001 attack, as President Obama addressed the nation and announced that bin Laden had been killed by American forces, Weddle started shaving.

"I spent my first five minutes crying and then I couldn't get it off fast enough," Weddle, 50, told *The Wenatchee World*.

"I wanted him to get rid of it, but it was his vow," his wife said. "I respected his passion and keeping a vow. I was willing to look past the beard because I love him. He looks 10 years younger. It's a very happy moment for us. It's a very happy moment for the whole nation."

Dan Wheat / Associated Press

CHAPTER 3: **HUNTING A TERRORIST**

Carie Lemack lost her mother, Judy Laroque, on Flight 11 on September 11, 2001. Listening to the president's announcement that bin Laden had been killed brought with it a mix of emotions.

"To now know the man who plotted and executed her murder is gone, it brings a

justified in honoring the efforts of those who carried out the battle but added: "You really shouldn't celebrate the death of anybody."

For an intelligence community that had endured its share of mistakes and failures over the past decade, bin Laden's killing

sense of relief, because we know other families don't have to suffer the same way we have and continue to do," she said.

Kathy Murphy, who watched the scene near the White House, said she was conflicted. She said bin Laden had caused so much suffering that the crowd was

brought redemption. For the military, it was an undeniable success. For the president, it was a national security victory.

The end of bin Laden brought with it a rare chance for a new beginning in America.

America Triumphs 91

Pakistani soldiers stand guard on top of a building at the hideout of al-Qaeda leader Osama bin Laden after his death by US Special Forces in a ground operation in Abbottabad on May 2, 2011. Pakistan said that the killing of Osama bin Laden in a US operation was a 'major setback' for terrorist organisations and a 'major victory' in the country's fight against militancy.

Intelligence Gathering

While Americans revel in the fact that notorious terrorist Osama bin Laden is dead, U.S. security agencies know there's no time to sit back and relax.

The clock is ticking for those agencies to analyze, dissect and act upon intelligence gathered in the raid on bin Laden's compound. Authorities believe the information could lead to more targeted killings—as soon as this year—and throw the Afghanistan war insurgency into disarray.

The Navy SEALs, who stormed bin Laden's Pakistan hideout, recovered several computers and other items — reportedly up to 10 hard drives and more than 100 storage devices. Authorities are hopeful they will uncover leads that expose al-Qaeda leaders and networks.

Marine Maj. Gen. Richard Mills said: "I think the intelligence gathered off the site of the [bin Laden] hit will have a tremendous impact. I think it will identify people who are providing, again, material support to the insurgency in Afghanistan. I think it will provide targets to be worked. And I think it'll have a tremendous impact a little bit later in the year as the loss of that leadership begins to take place and they lose those capabilities."

Don Borelli, a former counterterrorism special agent with the FBI, characterized the data mining going on now as the "calm before the storm."

"I've spoken to some of my colleagues in the bureau and they're not going crazy jumping through hoops yet," he said. "It's going to happen relatively soon because once they get that data in a format that can be manipulated and exploited (they'll act on it)."

Unearthing information about active plots is the highest priority.

"The way you approach a treasure trove of information like this is to go at it in priority order. What you want to find first and fastest is any indication of plots actively under way," said John McLaughlin, former deputy director at the CIA.

Within a week of the attack on bin Laden, the United States had already acted on intelligence gathered at the compound. On May 5, 2011, U.S. Department of Homeland Security released a notice tied to rail security saying that, in February 2010, al-Qaeda members discussed a plan to derail U.S. trains by placing obstructions on tracks. The plan was to coincide with the 10th anniversary of the September 11 attacks.

Some intelligence officials fear that discovery may be the the tip of the iceberg of potential plots.

So, while the nation celebrates its triumph over bin Laden, security and intelligence officers dig in even deeper, hoping to protect the United States from further terror.

Burial at Sea

Why was terrorist Osama bin Laden buried at sea?

The morning after he was killed, Pentagon officials said bin Laden's body was handled in accordance with Muslim traditions, which include strict rules on burial taking place within 24 hours after death.

Sources confirmed that his body was released into the sea in a weighted bag from a U.S. Navy vessel on Monday, likely into the North Arabian Sea.

White House officials said they had decided prior to the killing that, if bin Laden died during the attack, they would bury him at sea in order to prevent his grave from becoming a shrine for his followers. They planned to include all rites associated with Muslim burials, the

official said.

"The disposal of—the burial of—bin Laden's remains was done in strict conformance with Islamic precepts and practices," said John O. Brennan, President Barack Obama's top counterterrorism adviser.

"It was prepared in accordance with the Islamic requirements," he said. "We early on made provisions for that type of burial, and we wanted to make sure that it was going to be done, again, in strict conformance. So it was taken care of in the appropriate way."

After the fact, Islamic scholars and clerics were divided over whether the sea burial was appropriate or an insult to Muslims. Some said bin Laden should have been buried on land in a simple grave.

Osama's body was brought to the USS CVN-70 Carl Vinson for his sea burial.

CHAPTER 4

THE NATION, WORLD REACT

Pride. Hope. Shock, Fear. Confusion. Anger. Elation. Concern.

Reaction to the news of Osama bin Laden's death elicited a range of emotions from both Americans and those around the world.

Many individuals admitted feeling

The New York Post: GOT HIM!
Chicago Tribune: US KILLS BIN LADEN
Philadelphia Enquirer: BIN LADEN DEAD
The Washington Post: JUSTICE HAS BEEN DONE
New York Daily News: ROT IN HELL!

conflicted about the killing of America's Public Enemy No. 1. He had killed or masterminded the killing of thousands of people, but should a death be celebrated?

News of his death brought with it the hope that a page has been turned on the War on Terror, but also warnings that the fight was far from over.

Newspapers across the United States ran bold, often 6-column headlines, proclaiming the news:

While large, spontaneous celebrations erupted near the White House and Ground Zero, other, smaller gatherings took place across the United States. Many of today's college students were still in elementary school the day the Twin Towers fell, but that didn't stop them from gathering to salute the significance of the United States finally bringing the mastermind of those attacks to justice. Impromptu gatherings burst out on

U.S. Leaders React

News of bin Laden's demise elicited official comments from many U.S. leaders. Here are a few:

"Earlier this evening, President Obama called to inform me that American forces killed Osama bin Laden, the leader of the al-Qaeda network that attacked America on September 11, 2001. I congratulated him and the men and women of our military and intelligence communities who devoted their lives to this mission. They have our everlasting gratitude. This momentous achievement marks a victory for America, for people who seek peace around the world, and for all those who lost loved ones on September 11, 2001. The fight against terror goes on, but tonight America has sent an unmistakable message: No matter how long it takes, justice will be done."

—Former President George W. Bush

"I congratulate the president, the national security team and the members of our armed forces on bringing Osama bin Laden to justice after more than a decade of murderous al-Qaeda attacks."

—Former President Bill Clinton

"This is great news for the security of the American people and a victory in our continued fight against al-Qaeda and radical extremism around the world. We continue to face a complex and evolving terrorist threat, and it is important that we remain vigilant in our efforts to confront and defeat the terrorist enemy and protect the American people. I want to congratulate—and thank—the hard-working men and women of our Armed

Forces and intelligence community for their tireless efforts and perseverance that led to this success. I also want to commend President Obama and his team, as well as President Bush, for all of their efforts to bring Osama bin Laden to justice."

— House Speaker John Boehner, R-Ohio.

"The death of Osama bin Laden marks the most significant development in our fight against al-Qaeda. I salute President Obama, his national security team, Director Panetta, our men and women in the intelligence community and military, and other nations who supported this effort for their leadership in achieving this major accomplishment. It is a testament to the professionalism of our dedicated national security professionals that no American lives were lost in this operation.

"As we approach the 10th anniversary of the 9/11 attacks, I hope that today's action provides some comfort to the 9/11 families who lost loved ones in the devastating attacks on our shores.

"Though the death of Osama bin Laden is historic, it does not diminish our relentless pursuit of terrorists who threaten our country."

—House Democratic Leader Nancy Pelosi of California

"Osama bin Laden is dead, killed in a targeted U.S. operation authorized by President Obama.

"This is the most significant victory in our fight against al-Qaeda and terrorism, but that fight is not over. We will continue to support our troops and the American civilians who are fighting every day to protect our homeland.

"Nine-and-a-half years ago, Osama bin Laden masterminded the horrific attacks against the United States that killed nearly 3,000 people. As we remember those who were killed on that dark day in September and their families, we also reaffirm our resolve to defeat the terrorist forces that killed them and thousands of others across the globe. Because of courageous Americans in our military and intelligence community, their leader is now gone."

—Senate Majority Leader Sen. Harry Reid, D-Nev.

campuses across the country, from the University of Maryland to Iowa State University to Ohio State University.

Outside the United States, reaction was quick but mixed.

Throughout much of the Middle East, news of bin Laden's killing was greeted with relief and anticipation that life there would improve.

"Bin Laden's acts robbed us of freedom to talk and move around," said Mohammad al-Mansouri in the United Arab Emirates. "He turned us into targets at home and suspects in every foreign country we traveled to."

"This is the fate that evil killers deserve," said outgoing Lebanese Prime Minister Saad Hariri, deploring the harm that bin Laden did to "the image of Islam and Arab causes."

Iranian officials reacted to bin Laden's death with a blend of skepticism and political spin.

Foreign ministry spokesman Ramin Mehmanparast said: "We hope that this development will end war, conflict, unrest and the death of innocent people, and help to establish peace and tranquility in the region. This development clearly shows that there is no need for a major military deployment to counter one individual."

Reaction to bin Laden's death was less vocal in the Muslim world. Some fundamentalists were angry he was killed by U.S. commandos; others said they were anxious to put al-Qaeda and its violent acts behind them.

Afghan President Hamid Karzai said bin Laden had gotten what he deserved, but he scolded U.S. officials for ongoing civilian casualties there.

"Remember that the war against terrorism is not in the valleys and villages of Afghanistan, but in the terrorists training centers and camps. The fighting

US Vice President Joe Biden places a wreath at the 9/11 Memorial in the Pentagon in Washington, DC, on May 5, 2011, to honor the victims of the September 11, 2001 attacks.

should be taken there," Karzai said.

Reaction from European leaders to the killing of bin Laden was widely favorable.

"We woke up in a safer world," said Jerzy Buzek, president of the European

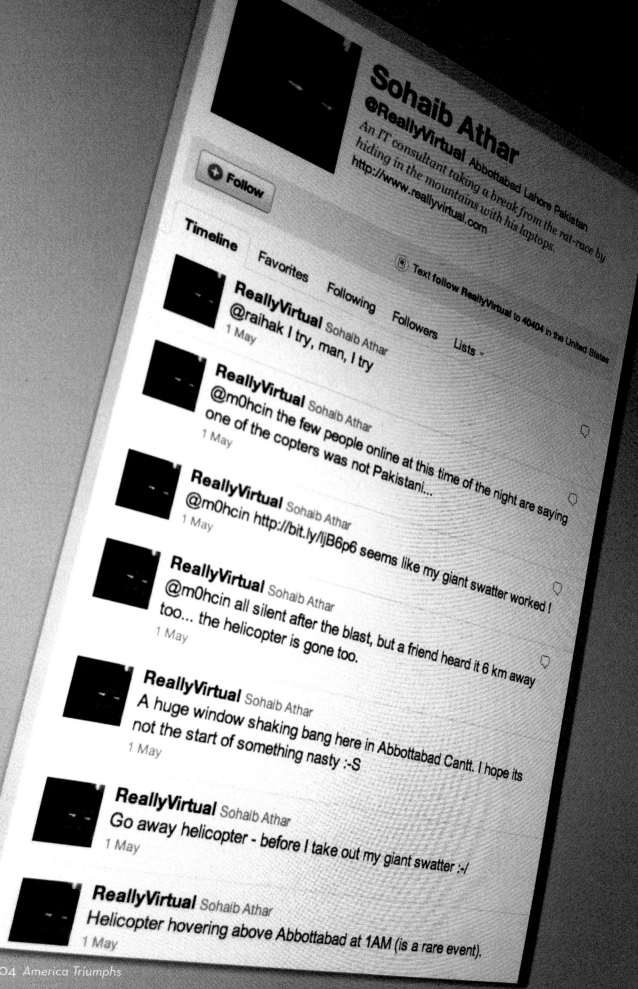

Sohaib Athar

@ReallyVirtual Abbottabad Lahore Pakistan
An IT consultant taking a break from the rat-race by
hiding in the mountains with his laptops.
http://www.reallyvirtual.com

⊕ **Follow**

Timeline   Favorites

Following   Followers   Lists ▾

📱 Text follow ReallyVirtual to 40404 in the United States

ReallyVirtual Sohaib Athar
@raihak I try, man, I try
1 May

ReallyVirtual Sohaib Athar
@m0hcin the few people online at this time of the night are saying
one of the copters was not Pakistani...
1 May

ReallyVirtual Sohaib Athar
@m0hcin http://bit.ly/ljB6p6 seems like my giant swatter worked !
1 May

ReallyVirtual Sohaib Athar
@m0hcin all silent after the blast, but a friend heard it 6 km away
too... the helicopter is gone too.
1 May

ReallyVirtual Sohaib Athar
A huge window shaking bang here in Abbottabad Cantt. I hope its
not the start of something nasty :-S
1 May

ReallyVirtual Sohaib Athar
Go away helicopter - before I take out my giant swatter :-/
1 May

ReallyVirtual Sohaib Athar
Helicopter hovering above Abbottabad at 1AM (is a rare event).
1 May

Tweeting the News

After a 10-year hunt for the world's most infamous terrorist, news of Osama bin Laden's death flooded Twitter with the highest number of tweets per second ever —around 3,000.

Social media analysis firm Crimson Hexagon reported that instant electronic reaction was a mix of fear, humor and solemn remembrance.

Using a special semantic analysis algorithm, tweets were categorized: positive or negative, humor or celebration, revulsion or sadness.

By May 3, 2011, the firm had divided tweets pertaining to the news into one of five categories:

29 percent of the messages were simply sharing the news that bin Laden was dead.

27 percent of the messages were humorous or sarcastic.

21 percent were celebratory messages.

12 percent of the tweets remembered lives lost.

11 percent of the messages mentioned fear of future retaliation.

Sohaib Athar, an IT contractor, was on holiday in Abbottabad in northern Pakistan in early May 2011. That's when he unwittingly became the guy who live-tweeted about the raid on bin Laden's compound. A selection of his Tweets:

@ ReallyVirtual:Helicopter hovering about Abbottabad at 1AM (a rare event).

@ ReallyVirtual:Go away helicopter – before I take out my giant swatter. :-/

@ ReallyVirtual:A huge window shaking bang here in Abbottabad Cantt, I hope it's not the start of something nasty. :-S

@ ReallyVirtual:The Abbottbad helicopter/UFO was shot down near the Bilal Town area, and there's report of a flash. People saying it could be a drone.

@ ReallyVirtual:And now a plane flying over Abbottabad …

@ ReallyVirtual:I guess Abbottabad is going to get as crowded as the Lahore I left behind for some peace and quiet. *sigh*

@ ReallyVirtual:Interesting rumors in the otherwise uneventful Abbottabad air today.

@ ReallyVirtual:Uh oh, now I'm the guy who liveblogged the Osama raid without knowing it.

Within hours, bin Laden's death was the subject of more than 2.2 million mentions on Twitter, but it certainly wasn't the only social media outlet to see a spike in activity May 1, 2011.

By Monday afternoon, there were 2.8 million tweets and nearly 74,000 blog mentions about the terrorist's death. The day after the shooting, Google Trends ranked "osama bin laden dead" as its most popular search in the United States.

Within two hours after reports first surfaced that bin Laden had been killed, a Facebook page titled OSAMA BIN LADEN IS DEAD had already accumulated more than 150,000 "likes."

Union Parliament. "Even if the fight of the international community against terrorists is not over, an important step in the fight against al-Qaeda has been made."

British Prime Minister David Cameron called bin Laden's death "a relief" and "a massive step forward in the fight against

able to report a success, but international terrorism has not been yet defeated," she said. "All of us will have to remain on alert. We shall remain vigilant and we shall continue to cooperate on an international level. What has become clear today is that there will be further successes in the fight

US President Barack Obama addresses troops at Fort Campbell, Kentucky, May 6, 2011 after he met and decorated the 'full assault force' behind the clandestine raid that killed Osama bin Laden.

terrorism."

German Chancellor Angela Merkel praised the U.S. military strike. She said that, although bin Laden said he was acting in the name of Islam, the truth was that "he despised the basic values of his and everybody else's religion."

At the same time, Merkel was quick to warn that the war on terrorism is far from over.

"Last night the forces of peace were

against terror, even if they take a long time to achieve, and the death of bin Laden is a huge success in this endeavor."

Within Africa, there was mixed reaction to bin Laden's death. The terrorist's deadliest strike in Africa was the 1998 bombing of the U.S. embassies in Kenya and Tanzania that together killed 224 people.

Kenyan President Mwai Kibaki called the al-Qaeda leader's death an "act of justice"

Talking to Kids About bin Laden

The morning after the U.S. military operation that killed terrorist Osama bin Laden, the world was abuzz with the news. Newspapers, television and radio news, the Internet ... even in the line at the supermarket ... everyone was discussing bin Laden's killing.

That prompted many schools and parenting experts to address a seemingly unanswerable question: How, if at all, to address the issue of bin Laden's death with children. Should our kids be celebrating his demise? Should they be less fearful after his death? What if they didn't know they were supposed to be fearful in the first place?

Dr. Robyn Silverman, nationally known child development specialist, says it's normal for children, parents and educators to be confused and anxious when faced with an issue that has no easy answers. Sure, your kids may not watch the news themselves, but don't fool yourself: they'll hear the news from friends or other media.

Silverman cautions, ready or not, it's important for adults to be available to children at times like these. She encourages parents to be accessible and honest, without over-sharing. Also, be quick to remind kids that adults are doing everything they can to make certain America is a safe place to live.

Similarly, developmental psychologist Marilyn Price-Mitchell says children should be allowed to share their thoughts and feelings about the news.

"Talk to your children about your feelings," she said. "Ask them about theirs. Perhaps they are too young to remember the day when the World Trade Center was attacked and the immense grief you felt. Tell them about that day. Talk about justice—and the consequences of our actions."

Price-Mitchell says the discussion doesn't have to center on bin Laden's death. It might, instead, be a good time to talk about American values and even family values.

"Families who create open environments for dialogue with children around values and meaning in life nurture kids who grow up to morally reason for themselves," she said.

New Yorkers react to news of the death of Osama bin Laden at the intersection of Church Street and Vesey Street at Ground Zero on the morning of May 2, 2011.

for the victims of the Nairobi bombing and commended all those involved in tracking down and killing bin Laden.

In Morocco, where the government blames an April 2011 bombing in Marrakech on an al-Qaeda affiliated group, Communications Minister Khalid Naciri said the entire world suffered at bin Laden's hands.

Uganda's government officials called bin Laden's death a "momentous event." Spokesman Fred Opolot pledged that Ugandan troops in an African Union force in Somalia would continue to fight the al-Qaeda-affiliated al-Shabaab militia. At the same time, an al-Shabaab spokesman threatened revenge attacks for bin Laden's death.

Anders Fogh Rasmussen, secretary-general of NATO, called the action "a significant success for the security of NATO allies and all the nations which have joined us in our efforts to combat the scourge of global terrorism."

Of course, not all political factions cheered bin Laden's killing. In Oakistan, where the al-Qaeda leader was killed, the main Taliban faction vowed to strike back.

"If he has been martyred, we will avenge his death and launch attacks against American and Pakistani governments and their security forces," said Ehsanullah Ehsan, the militant group's spokesman.

Afghan Taliban fighters mourned bin Laden's death.

"My heart is broken," said militant

US Marines of Regiment Combat Team 1 (RCT 1) watch TV as President Barack Obama announces the death of Osama bin Laden at Camp Dwyer in Helman Province. on May 2, 2011.

Mohebullah. "In the past, we heard a lot of rumors about his death, but if he did die, it is a disaster and a black day."

AMERICA TRIUMPHS: EPILOGUE

Heinrich Bernhard Ackermann. Douglas Brian Gurian. Vassilios G. Haramis. Clara Victorine Hinds. Irina Kolpakova. CeeCee Lyles. Arturo Angelo Sereno. Bonnie Jeanne Smithwick. LCDR Eric A. Cranford, USN. Yuguag Zheng.

These are but 10 of the 2,977 victims who lost their lives September 11, 2001, in the worst terrorist attack ever to take place on American soil. These people and those who died with them were mothers, fathers, sons and daughters. They left behind families, unborn children and friends whose lives will never be the same.

Many tears fell on September 11—and on the days that followed. Americans were sad and fearful and vulnerable. But we, as a nation, carried on.

Young men and women enlisted in a military dedicated to fighting against terrorism. We submitted to more thorough searches at airports and sports stadiums. We taught our children to walk the fine line between caution and fear.

We debated over whether a mosque should be built at Ground Zero and whether a pastor in Florida had the right to burn the Quran. We flew American flags where they had never flown before.

Then, nearly 10 long years later, we got word that U.S. Navy SEALs had found and killed the mastermind behind 9/11.

As a nation, we breathed a collective sigh of relief. Some partied while others prayed. Osama bin Laden was dead but we were not so naïve as to believe terrorism was too.

We will remain vigilant. We will remain hopeful. Above all, we will never forget.